CHOOSING HOW WE DIE

The Experiences Of Those Who Did

JUNE W. LAMB

BALBOA.
PRESS

A DIVISION OF HAY HOUSE

Balboa Press books may be ordered through booksellers or by contacting:

Balboa Press
A Division of Hay House
1663 Liberty Drive
Bloomington, IN 47403
www.balboapress.com
1 (877) 407-4847

Because of the dynamic nature of the Internet, any web addresses or links contained in this book may have changed since publication and may no longer be valid. The views expressed in this work are solely those of the author and do not necessarily reflect the views of the publisher, and the publisher hereby disclaims any responsibility for them.

The author of this book does not dispense medical advice or prescribe the use of any technique as a form of treatment for physical, emotional, or medical problems without the advice of a physician, either directly or indirectly. The intent of the author is only to offer information of a general nature to help you in your quest for emotional and spiritual well-being. In the event you use any of the information in this book for yourself, which is your constitutional right, the author and the publisher assume no responsibility for your actions.

Print information available on the last page.

ISBN: 978-1-5043-5125-6 (sc)
ISBN: 978-1-5043-5126-3 (e)

Library of Congress Control Number: 2016902989

Balboa Press rev. date: 04/14/2016

Also Available by June W. Lamb

"The Learning Journey"
Absorbing Life's Lessons

DEDICATION

I am very grateful to have received so much support, with encouragement to share what I have been taught about family systems, as well as about individual courage in facing our physical death. We have made a great leap in consciousness this past decade by passing laws to include physician assisted death, or death with dignity, as a choice when we can no longer sustain physical life.

I dedicate this book to the many friends and colleagues who know of my work in helping families dealing with catastrophic illness. By writing this book I have chosen to share yet another choice in how we die which I have been witness to. The stories of people who have chosen to be released from their physical body without anyone else giving assistance are remarkable. Having been given permission to share these stories, I offer their experiences and their families response to their choice in dying. They have made an invaluable contribution to our understanding and acceptance of our mortality.

"We run after values that, at death, become zero. At the end of your life, nobody asks how many degrees you have or how many mansions you built, or how many Rolls Royces you can afford. That's what dying patients teach you."

Dr. Elisabeth Kubler-Ross

ACKNOWLEDGEMENTS

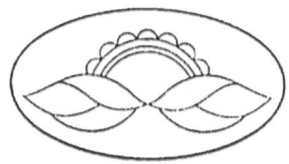

Every story in this book is true, but it has been necessary to change names and places in order to provide privacy. I am eternally grateful to those whose stories were used to illustrate a universally human experience, that of dying. I acknowledge the great privilege in having been a part of those stories. It has taken years of effort to discipline my use of time in order to complete this undertaking and I have received the generous support and encouragement of so many individuals along the way that it is difficult to name them all. However, they know who they are and I extend my gratitude for the time spent in reading, commenting and contributing to my endeavor to put down on paper this invaluable knowledge for the general public.

CONTENTS

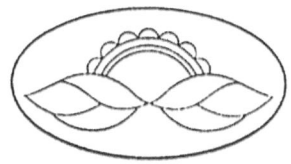

INTRODUCTION

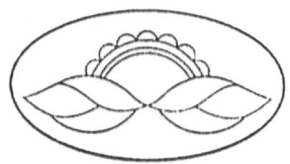

Discussing death is a huge problem in our culture. We fear death. We avoid discussing or planning for death or, often, even acknowledging the inevitability of our own physical death. Talking openly about our own mortality is often considered a morbid, paranoid way of thinking. The familiarity and reality of our surroundings and relationships in our present life often make us avoid talking about physical death because we don't want to leave the familiar.

For those suffering from what they have been told is an incurable disease or finding themselves living in a body that no longer functions, the failure to have considered their eventual death can have dire effects. If science has concluded that your physical life cannot be saved and you have never expressed your wishes about your dying process, you may be faced with a lingering, painful and expensive end to your physical life. Extraordinary changes in promoting longevity and prohibiting physical death have come about in the last 60 years and, unfortunately, many, many people are unaware of a choice that is not tied to financial profit or illegal activities. It does not involve the assistance of medical professionals or a deeply loved relative. California recently joined five other States that are allowing physician assisted physical death to be chosen. This choice requires "competency" of the terminal patient and several signatures from others who attest to and verify the dying patient's choice. This means that the decision cannot wait until the dying process is well advanced, but is something we can all consider while still able to accept our mortality and understand death with dignity. The national group that addresses the legality of assisted dying, Compassion and Choice, acknowledges this lesser known method of dying with the acronym VSED (Voluntarily Stopped Eating and Drinking).

In this book I have written about my own experiences in accompanying four people, my mother and three friends in my age group, who asked for my emotional support and protection from intervention in their dying process. I have written my observations of their journeys. They were not clients and I never received money from any of them. I was approached as a friend or relative and not as a professional therapist. As will be seen in the individual reports, the idea of stopping eating and drinking came directly from the dying patient.

We have acquired many new choices in the last millennium. We can now control when, with whom, or if we have babies. We can choose whether to get married by clergy or a deputized friend, as well as whether it will be in a church, a garden, or at the beach. We are also having funerals and life celebrations in a variety of places and spreading ashes of loved ones in lakes, back yards, or placing them in lockets to be worn by family members. The changes are coming swiftly and it seems only fair that a relatively unknown practice of choosing how we die be shared with the general public. This choice does not require action from another person and therefore avoids the label of "assisted suicide." It does not include agreement from a medical professional willing to participate by prescribing lethal drugs and so avoids "euthanasia" or felony charges where that is deemed illegal. Also, it allows you to free your loved ones from carrying a moral burden by asking them to make the decision to withdraw life support. Frequently, the family members do not agree and this disagreement can create long-standing resentment and bitterness among them. When choice is made by the dying patient and clearly communicated to loved ones, there is very little regret left with survivors and I have interviewed them after their loss to make certain this is the case. Compassionate use of pain medication and the fact that the body need not process nutrition seems to relieve the patient who makes this choice and most often results in a mildly euphoric and peaceful death.

Carrying a belief system acquired in childhood, which declares there is divine punishment and hell after death, can paralyze us when faced with our impending physical death. For some, learning the manner of dying discussed here opens the fear that someone will force death on others for their own convenience. However, in states that allow assisted euthanasia, this fear is not supported by any data.

The truth is that when the reality of death has been faced, life takes on new meaning. When we realize the magic and reality of having a body in which to operate, we will treat that body with great care. We will treasure each day as an opportunity to proceed with our passions at a physical level, to give back our talent and to savor nature's incredible dependability. Science has discovered that there is a different life expectancy for all biological forms of life, but this does not exclude accidents, pandemics, or poor lifestyle. Life expectancy in the United States has risen dramatically in the last fifty years, adding years to most people's lives.

Whether death has occurred to a child, or to a very old person, it may always seem too short a lifetime. The truth that we are very vulnerable as biological organisms does not seem to prevent us from taking incredible risks or to be thoughtless as to our transient existence. Our body gives us the ability to verbally communicate, to show affection and to enjoy exercise. Christopher Reeves left us with the undeniable model of productivity and contribution when our body no longer functions normally but our mind and emotions are intact. Although confined to an iron lung, he continued to make a difference in the world.

As a practicing psychotherapist, I have trained and worked closely with hospice volunteers to help families facing the death of a family member. From these experiences, I know how rarely people spend time considering their own deaths or make known their plans as to how they would like their lives to end. I have observed how very helpful it is to supporting families to have had time to discuss these plans when in health or when they accept an impending death. Giving their family members the opportunity to carry out their wishes is the last gift the dying family member can give to those they leave behind, although the surviving family will still experience shock and grief. Anyone reading this writing is terminal. Those who have a diagnosis of cancer or are fighting a catastrophic illness certainly may expect to die sooner than their neighbors or other family members. But even without a serious illness, there is no certainty that we will survive any day. Our vulnerability is accompanied by the comfort of knowing that we live in a miraculously efficient body that can heal, regenerate, reconstruct and survive many challenges.

The stories included in this writing came to me from acquaintances simply seeking a dialog. Their need in seeking a communication was not necessarily due to defeat or because they were suicidal. Their conclusion nearly always came from a sense of triumph and satisfaction with accomplishments and seeing nothing but suffering and uselessness ahead. It is because I was given the privilege of accompanying some who made that choice that I wrote the following chapters.

The direction of my own life brought the difficulty of accepting the permanence of death to my attention at a very early age. In my book titled <u>The Learning Journey</u>, I share several of my personal challenges which were traumatic and required periods of grief. These personal traumas crystallized my goal of becoming a professional who could help families facing the death of a family member. Those families have also been my teachers.

I am forever grateful to our citizens who devote their lives to the science of medicine and take on the role of healers such as doctors and nurses. Their commitment to their profession is a gift from which we all benefit. In this writing, I am not unconscious of the lives saved and the sacrifices made by these dedicated health professionals. I wish only to address citizens facing the fact that when science cannot save the patient and the choice is between that of a lingering, painful, expensive death or a conscious decision to stop feeding a body that cannot be healed. Many doctors will continue curative treatment when they know it cannot save the patient because the decision makers for that patient disagree and insist on keeping their loved one alive. Some families facing loss can be ignorant of the existing choices, or the doctor may be unwilling to make it clear that death is approaching. Therefore the choice of palliative care or ending nutrition and hydration is not considered.

When we look at the current thrust in our evolution, it is clear that this topic has been growing in importance for some time. In my own mother's case, expectations for the period of history in which she lived were for women to live as satellites to their husbands' needs and wishes. Her life centered on her goals of keeping my father comfortable, well fed and free of worries from the children's activities. When he died, she was unable to restructure her life by pursuing goals for herself and never stopped grieving for him.

When she began to experience cardiac arrests, she almost welcomed the fact that her death might be near. This did not depress her. When she regained consciousness, after experiencing a second cardiac arrest, and found a pace maker attached externally to her chest, she looked down at it and demanded that it be removed. Since the hospital in which she was being cared for had a policy of implanting a pace maker if the patient had the possibility of one more year of life, they refused to remove it. My older sister, who had worked as a law practitioner, gathered her peers and they created a legal paper demanding the pace maker be removed that had to be signed by our mother in the presence of an attorney and her doctor. After the signings had taken place, and after the removal of the pace maker, she was moved to a private room where she died three days later. I talked with her during those three days and detected only a deep satisfaction in her expectation of meeting our father again. As her daughter, I am grateful that the status and independence of women has changed greatly in the past 50 years.

It is only recently that we have achieved the skills of bringing people back to life who have been clinically dead. The similarity of the reports by people who have been brought back to life about that "place" they experienced while clinically dead have been written about recently by famous authors. Two of them, Dr. Eben Alexander and Amy Berman, have debunked long-held beliefs about the afterlife. Another book that outlines the changes taking place is Knocking on Heaven's Door by Katy Butler. Everyone should read her immaculate research on how our present dilemma developed.

An Example of New Thinking

A doctor once called on me as a professional family therapist to ask if I would come to the hospital to talk with the family of his patient who was dying. The doctor's frustration came from his observation that the patient's room always included at least one family member, and in the evening several more would arrive with balloons and cheerful social conversation. "Lou's weight is below 100 lbs. and we expected him to die last week. Can you talk to his family about this process?" the doctor asked.

I arrived at the hospital that evening to find a very frail, pale man lying in his hospital bed as six others in the room chatted with one another. I explained my need to speak with the patient and the others went out to the lounge in the hallway.

"Lou, you appear to be very weak. Is your pain well controlled and do you wish this activity around you to continue?"

Lou's answer was prompt. "I'm really ready to die, but I don't want to miss the party. They are so supportive of me and I don't want to disappoint them."

"So you are comfortable enough and enjoying their company for as long as you can?"

"No. I just don't seem to be able to die."

I left his room and went out to talk with the family who were waiting outside. I told them of his consternation in disappointing them and also that we know a dying person sometimes needs time alone to process their journey. One by one they returned to his room and spent a few minutes telling him of their love and their acceptance that his body could no longer sustain life. Each of them came back to the lounge in tears and when they had all had their moment to say goodbye, they retired to the cafeteria for a last cup of coffee and mutual support. Lou died about 2 a.m. the next morning. They later sent me a note of thanks. It was signed by nine family members.

CHAPTER I
CHARLIE

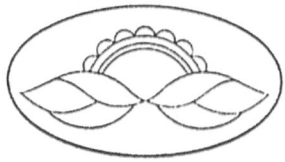

In a recent case, a friend had been told there was no cure for his rare blood disease. He had been diagnosed with myelodysplastic syndrome that progressed to leukemia when he was 84. Knowing that he had no patience with the curative treatments being offered, he chose to use supportive therapies only. When he became unresponsive to the supportive medications and his condition continued to deteriorate, he and the family were advised that death might occur within six months. By now, Charlie was 86 years old and had led an exceptionally successful life. Upon hearing his prognosis, he announced to his doctor that he was unwilling to be treated by any medical means that would prolong his life. He was willing to continue the blood transfusions as long as he was experiencing some quality time with his family. He was put on a waiting list for a bed in a nearby Veteran's Hospital Hospice unit.

We had known of each other in the community but were not well acquainted. He called me because he knew I had specialized in working with families dealing with catastrophic illness. His home was only a short distance away so I agreed to pay him a social visit after being informed that he was on hospice care for his blood disease. Our first visit lasted 3 hours and we never stopped being amazed at how similar our thinking was about the big depression, the second world war and current politics. I began to visit him in his home as a friend about every other day, thereby becoming acquainted with his son, who was visiting from another State, and his daughter who lived nearby.

Although sad at the thought of his physical absence from their lives, his children promised him that they would follow his wishes. They agreed that there would be no heroic measures to extend his life and that he would be included in all decisions regarding his care as long as he was able. Because he was quite well known, he chose to keep the news of his impending death from public knowledge until the transfusions he was receiving began to lose their effectiveness. When he agreed to make the state of his health public knowledge, he experienced a deluge of visitors and felt energized by their presence. About that time, a bed at the

Veteran's hospital hospice unit became available and he was moved to that facility. His loyal friends followed him and for another two weeks he enjoyed the total care and warmth of the staff who took care of him.

Because they were no longer effective, the blood transfusions were stopped, and with the use of drugs he was pain free for a time. He became physically weaker and weaker although he was completely mentally awake and aware. When the nurses could no longer get him out of bed to use the rest room and he was told of their plan to catheterize him, Charlie suddenly announced that he would not receive further visitors. He spoke with one of the hospice physicians and announced that he was ready to die and wanted to stop eating and drinking. She informed him that it would not help him die any time soon, and would probably take a few weeks. This is not backed by research. They continued to bring food trays three times a day in case he "changed his mind." He stared at the television with no sound for hours and days, his mind active and aware, but too weak to communicate.

His daughter insisted they turn him on his side, and give him the morphine that the doctor had authorized. The head nurse decided that the dose the doctor recommended was too strong, and called him, convincing him to cut the dose in half. When his daughter asked why, the nurse informed her that it could suppress his breathing. When she asked what difference it made if the death he was hoping for came a few hours earlier, she was told that they wanted him to have a "natural death." He was very restless, and without the energy to swallow fluids, he slipped into a light coma. One night later I received a phone call from his daughter. She was very upset because the nurses who cared for him were trying to coax him from his coma to give him liquid nourishment through a straw in the corner of his mouth.

"June, I asked them to stop, but they insist that he should have a natural death."

"Go back to those nurses and tell them they are thwarting God's will. . . that it is Charlie's decision to let go of his physical body," I replied.

When a new nurse came on duty she assured Charlie's daughter that she would make sure he was comfortable, not in pain, and that the end was near. His daughter was fearful that all of his caregivers might not agree and so stayed by his bedside through the entire night. I joined her at 7 a.m. the next day and took her place at his bedside while she went to nap in the empty visitor's lounge. Several times, a nurse would hesitate at the door to his room, but upon seeing me there, moved on down the hall. Three hours later his daughter shuffled into the room and saw that he was peacefully resting and after telling him once again how much she loved him, left to go home for a few hours. I stayed the rest of the day, gently stroking his arm and forehead as he slipped slowly into a very profound coma. His daughter came back one more time and smiled as she saw his visible comfort. After a few moments, she said that she felt satisfied his coma was very, very deep, that she had no unfinished business with him so would go back home. I, too, left late in the afternoon. Half an hour after reaching home, I received a phone call telling me he had died. Charlie's son soon arrived and two weeks later a community celebration of Charlie's life was held with hundreds of attendees.

Five months later, when I found that the choice of how we die was being examined in many publications on both the East and West Coasts, I decided to share my experiences. In order to add to our knowledge of feelings regarding this choice, I set about interviewing family survivors who had accompanied a relative who had chosen to die.

5 MONTHS LATER – THE INTERVIEW

I approached Charlie's adult daughter because I feel it is important to know what the survivors of a relative who had made the choice for death felt some time after their absence.

I first asked her, "How did you learn that your Dad was choosing to stop eating and drinking in order to die?" Her answer came quickly and willingly. She reviewed the year previous to his death, which had included a severe bladder infection, followed by pneumonia.

"After recovering from the pneumonia it was discovered that he was severely anemic and he began receiving blood transfusions. Upon further testing, his doctor discovered that he had a fatal type of leukemia. The pneumonia came back and he began coughing up blood. At this point, he called me and my brother together and announced his wishes: 'I don't believe in life after death and I don't want to screw around. I'm setting up my finances so you can pay the bills but I don't want to die here in my home.'

"Following his wishes, his doctor had put his name on the list for a bed in the hospice wing of the Veteran's Hospital. Dad continued writing his newspaper column and enjoyed socializing as much as his energy would allow. Time between transfusions became shorter and shorter and he began suffering severe pain from infections that he was no longer able to fight due to his disease. He was receiving high doses of steroids that led to developing diabetes and all of its side effects. My brother and I both accompanied him when he was transferred to the Hospice unit at the hospital. We immediately communicated his acceptance of death to his doctors at the new facility as he became weaker and weaker. A public announcement regarding his state of health had brought dozens of people to his bedside at home and they followed him to the hospital. Their attention was a great stimulant and for a few days Dad sat up and enjoyed their support. When he was about to be catheterized he declared this was the last straw and made clear that it was his decision to stop eating and drinking."

I asked his daughter about her initial reaction upon hearing this. She did not hesitate and quickly replied that she had already accepted the inevitability of his death. She felt he had lived a good life, and was leaving nothing undone. She added:

"There is a time for death. One of the last things we did was reconcile the differences we had had in my adolescence and early adulthood. We had no unfinished business."

I asked, "Was this the first time you had known that someone could choose to die rather than continue curative treatment?"

"Yes, I hadn't had such an experience. When my grandfather passed away, I had taken a class on death and dying taught by Elisabeth Kubler-Ross. I had learned about all the differences in the way different cultures handle death. The movie "Gramps" had impressed me deeply. It helped when I was facing my father's death."

"Did he ever ask for your agreement regarding his decisions?" I asked.

"No, he didn't ask for family agreement but he had a signed 'Do Not Resuscitate' that was in place. He hated seeing my tears but I told him he didn't have to hang around for my sake. I told him to do what he needed to do."

"Did any health professionals ever try to stop your father from carrying out his decision?"

"My brother and I both saw him losing his ability to move. He kept trying to tell medical personnel that he was ready to die but they gave him spiritual advice and kept offering help. They never agreed that he could stop eating and drinking to hasten death. As he communicated less and less, I stepped in and asked for more pain control and also asked that his position be changed more often so that he was comfortable. I told them I was committed to helping him with this transition and hastening his death in any way I could. He had made this wish very, very clear. The nurses responded that they didn't want to be responsible for his death or to do anything illegal. I told them 'it is not illegal to stop eating and drinking or to give him morphine as prescribed.' I really believe their religious beliefs led them to continue trying to give him nourishment and I had to stay by his bed all night to protect him from their efforts to keep him alive. I was really grateful when you turned up at 7 a.m. and relieved me from this vigil."

"Did you ever see him wavering on his part regarding his decision?"

"Never."

"Did you ever experience any regret or anger that he took this path and didn't fight to stay alive?"

"I only experienced sadness and a growing awareness of loss."

"Looking back, would you have changed anything?"

"No. It would have been more helpful if the hospice help at the hospital had been more willing to follow his wishes.

The doctors in that unit are on rotation so we were dependent on the nursing staff."

"Was his decision a help or a hindrance in your grief process?"

"Because I was following his wishes, it made my grief process easier. I felt that having experienced anticipatory grief, I am a much wiser woman. There was no short cutting. The natural dying process has to go through known steps."

"Do you think you would follow his example under similar circumstances?"

"Yes. I would make very sure that my support, both medical professionals and family, understood my wishes. A misplaced trust in the doctor or nurses can be a surprise to the patient."

"Have you shared your experience of your father's choice with others? If you have, how did they react?"

"I haven't shared it with a lot of people, only family. My great uncle does not have a problem with this and has offered no push back."

"So you are at peace with this choice when doctors cannot cure an illness?"

"Yes. It helped a lot to have had many conversations when we were in previous crises and knew all the possibilities for keeping his life going. He came to terms with all the conditions under which he wished to stay alive. This was not the same as dying from dehydration when you are in perfect health. It makes it very different when you are dying from an incurable illness. All three of us agreed with his chosen manner of dying."

CHAPTER II
DENISE

Denise and I were long time friends. One morning, when Denise was 79 years old, she called and asked me to have lunch. I had no idea, other than the fact that we enjoyed each other's company, of what she was about to tell me. She told me she had just received a diagnosis of colon cancer from her doctor. It was his recommendation that she have immediate surgery to be followed by aggressive chemotherapy.

Denise was all too familiar with the serious nature of these procedures because of her work in the hospital. After careful thought she had decided not to have any medical intervention for her stage 3 colon cancer. When we met for lunch she went over the plans she had made. I listened with mixed feelings as she outlined her decision to die. Rather than face a long, drawn-out treatment plan which would include extended recovery phases as well as the strong possibility of death, she carefully detailed her wishes to me and was only asking if she had thought of everything. She also commented on her concern at spending thousands of dollars on what she considered the fruitless attempt to live longer.

At first, my thoughts centered on the reality of losing one of my best friends and the hole it would leave in my life. She made it clear that she was not looking for sympathy and was not ready to extend hers as she continued speaking.

"I am going to get a hospital bed placed at home where I can see my garden and ask a retired nurse that I know to move into my spare room. I have not spoken to her yet, but I'm sure that she can provide the pain control my doctor will prescribe. Then I will stop eating and drinking. As I said, I'm not asking you for an opinion, but I know you have dealt with many cancer patients and might think of something I need to do that I haven't thought of."

Taking a deep breath, I forced myself to focus on her immediate need. I began by saying that we must not leave any unfinished business that complicates the grief of our family when we die. Have you given thought to your legal papers, a will, a durable power of attorney? Will you tell Luke and Debra what you are telling me? Do you want to be involved in planning a funeral or an obituary? Are you going to get support from a hospice team and will your health care providers be supportive of your plan?"

She answered slowly. "I know that once I have stopped eating and drinking, death could occur within 8 to 12 days so I don't think I need hospice. Yes, I am going to tell my children exactly what is happening. I just hope they don't fight me on this. Since you know them both, I might need to have them talk to you if they have a conflict with it. I don't expect it to be too difficult because we have all talked about death a lot since their father died and they know that I am not afraid of it. Of course I may die very quickly because the cancer is already spreading."

Her friend who was the retired nurse agreed to move into the guest room of her home in order to be available for pain management. Denise asked if I could plan to stay over night with her occasionally to give her friend a break. A few days later I arrived with my belongings and her friend left to spend a night in her apartment. Denise smiled smugly and reported that she had not eaten or taken liquids for nearly three days. From everything I could observe, she was clean, comfortable and was still able to go from her bed to the easy chair by the window. Her lack of nutrition and hydration seemed to have made her somewhat euphoric.

The next morning she seemed very weak and did not want to move to the window chair. It was clear that she was rapidly losing strength. I talked with her son and he said that he and his sister would be over that evening. Later that morning Denise looked up at me and said, "I want a popsicle." I did not hesitate to get a popsicle from the kitchen freezer and Denise sucked on it with pleasure, handing the stick back to me when it was less than half gone. That evening her children arrived and although she was very sleepy, they had an amiable visit. Her friend returned and took up her skills in administering pain medication.

On the eighth day of her fast, Denise was clearly in the dying process. Both of her children returned and I spent the evening with them, sharing our memories of their mother and her many adventures. She had the support of her family and many friends because they all loved her and knew that her decisions were based upon her factual knowledge and her spiritual beliefs. She died two days later. The memorial service held in her church was attended by many, some of whom understood her choice to die without further treatment, and some who did not.

SEVEN YEARS LATER - THE INTERVIEW
WITH DENISE'S SON

It has been seven years since Denise's death and I still can hear what she would say if she was alive, regarding current events in our world. It was with great pleasure that I had a reason to approach her two children for the following interviews.

Luke is very busy in his profession as a licensed clinical social worker and school counselor serving a large high school district. So we decided to do the interview on the phone one evening when we were both free. We agreed that our goal was to widen the knowledge of the general public or anyone reading this writing as to whether making a personal choice to leave their physical body leaves our loved ones with regret or anger. The first question was posed to discover how Denise's survivors first learned of her decision to reject medical treatment. Luke answered with positive enthusiasm, making it clear that he had given his mother's manner of death a great deal of thought.

"She let us know she had cancer and wasn't going to have months and months of surgery and treatment. I assumed the pain would take over and she would accept opiates. The part of not eating came up later. A nurse explained that the pain meds would eventually inhibit the appetite but she didn't realize Mom had made the choice to stop eating. I knew death was coming but I thought the morphine would slow everything down. My initial reaction was one of relief that she was not going to suffer indefinitely. I had given the issue of death a great deal of thought even though I am only in my 40s. My Dad had died ten years earlier of leukemia.

"When Mom said 'I have cancer and it's going to kill me,' I knew she had given it a lot of thought. She was fine with the mysteries of what happens after death – she had accepted many Buddhist principles. That made it easier for us because she was clearly at peace with death. Also, she had experienced her mother's death. Grandma Ellen was very strong, and though she had already experienced many traumas, she was pissed that she was dying. She and Mom had had a somewhat hostile relationship. Mom had written a couple of articles about euthanasia and knew the controversy that surrounded it. Her mother did not have an 'easy death.'

"My sister and I had been aware of Mom's views when my father died. When she knew she was dying, Mom invited all her friends to come over for a visit, telling some her plans and just visiting with others. My sister and I kept in touch and communicated with each other constantly."

Continuing with my list of questions, I asked Luke if he had ever actually known anyone who chose to die by refusing food and drink.

"No, but I was very familiar with crisis because I had worked as a deputy sheriff in Wyoming and seen a lot of suicides or accidental deaths. I had also read Dr. Kevorkian's theory and I believe him to be a visionary and a prophet. I think that big pharma and big medical authority are the cause of Kevorkian's demonization.

"I don't think Mom had to deal with anyone trying to stop her from carrying out her decision. She believed in Kaiser Permanente and felt other private hospitals sometimes put money as their highest value rather than the patient's experience.

"I had returned to the Bay Area in 2003 so I had spent much more time with her in recent years and I saw her adjusting to what she could do and what she could no longer do as she aged. We communicated well.

"After she told me her plans, my first response was, 'Really, Mom?' She said 'yes' and I accepted it. I think it is easier when someone is 79 and not in their 40's to contemplate their death. I had also studied and practiced Buddhism so we were both at peace."

I was very moved in listening to this narration and yet wondered if he had had any regret or anger that they did not fight for more life.

"No, I haven't had any anger but I have thought of some things I would like to ask her. I think that would happen no matter how someone died. The fact that Mom took care of all her business and made most arrangements regarding her illness and approaching death made things really easy for us. I would not have changed anything except you do always want more time. Buddhism emphasizes the impermanence of physical life pointing out that pain can be relieved and alleviated, but change is constant. It is very comforting.

"She was very satisfied with her life lived, and that helped. Her plan was to go out honorably and not make everyone else suffer unnecessarily. I hope I could make a similar decision in those circumstances and not make my kids stop their lives to take care of me. In sharing this experience with others, I feel I am contributing in helping people find a new way of accompanying a dying family member.

"My sister and I are both very much on the same page regarding mother's death, knowing that there have always been illnesses that we cannot cure."

EIGHT YEARS LATER – INTERVIEW WITH DENISE'S DAUGHTER

"How did you first learn that your mother was choosing to stop eating and drinking in order to die?"

"The first shock was in knowing that she had cancer. But when she said she wasn't going to have any treatment – my response was, 'Really?' I was very surprised that she was not going to do anything, but it didn't take me long to come to the side of her thinking. It was clear that she didn't want to go through radiation or chemotherapy and the cancer was already stage 3.

"I wasn't aware at first that she was going to stop eating and drinking, but I expected that it would not be a long illness because of the stage at which it was diagnosed. My daughter and I went on a little trip with Mom after the diagnosis and when we went out to dinner, she ate very little and was clearly uncomfortable.

"I never tried to get her to change her mind about treatment because my Mom always had a really good sense of who she was and what she wanted. But I didn't really feel ready to let her go. I think I was feeling what they call survivor's guilt. But I knew she meant what she was saying when she called in her Priest and they worked on her memorial service.

"It was great to have that time with her, even though I knew that she would die soon. Now I sometimes wish I had spent more time with her but I think it would never have been enough. I remember my son coming to visit her, sitting on the chair by her bed about a week before she died. He played his guitar for her. It gave all of us a great sense of satisfaction and peace.

"I've talked about our experience with other people who have a similar situation – a relative who is terminally ill. They have been very interested because this choice is still new and I think it's important to share my experience. When Mom first told me about the cancer I said, 'Wait a minute, I thought you would live to be ninety.' But then we talked about the quality of life. When others tell me about the struggle they have in caring for an elderly parent with dementia, I say 'Thank you, Mom.' She made sure we didn't have to do that. Some people have to stop their own lives to take care of parents and that doesn't seem the natural order of things. She wanted her death to have dignity."

I was very absorbed in listening to Debra's thoughts and especially when she brought up the natural order of life. I quickly replied: "You are right. If you watch nature, you will see that parents do not continue to be responsible for or ask to be authority for their progeny. Coyotes teach cubs to hunt and fish and then leave them on their own. In the bird world, a parent will push a chick out of the nest if they do not fly away on their own when they have reached maturity."

Debra and I found we had developed a very similar view of death. She replied: "I think it's important that people talk about and deal with the reality of death.

"I teach fourth graders and I try to teach them by raising trout in the classroom. When some of the eggs didn't hatch and when some of the young trout died, we had a chance to talk about life and death in nature."

"I think that's wonderful – that you bring all that into the classroom and make it a part of the whole picture. There are some who never really have the chance to consider death until later in life."

"I think it's much easier to grasp the truth of life and death when you are young. My husband's stepmother has had a very hard time accepting his father's death and no matter how we try to help her, she tries to hang on and act as though he is still living.

"I really don't like the idea of suicide, but that wasn't a part of what my Mom was doing. Suicide wasn't involved in her choosing how to die. She knew that her cancer was advanced and she knew too much about her chances of surviving surgery and radiation or chemotherapy. More or less, she chose to let nature take its course. I'm not sure she talked to me as she did to you, but as a parent I know there are some things you try to protect your kids from. I think she was torn between being very honest about what was happening to her and not wanting my brother and me to endure the process. Mom also had some groups she met with where they discussed spiritual things.

"When it was close to the end, my brother would be with her on Saturday and I would be there on Sunday. She died very, very early on a Sunday morning but he waited until daybreak to call me. I knew I needed to go there, even though she was dead. I sat beside her body talking to her and I felt her spirit. I'm so glad I was able to do that.

"We all had a sense that this was the end. I feel I had the chance to say 'goodbye' in very special ways."

CHAPTER III
SOPHIA

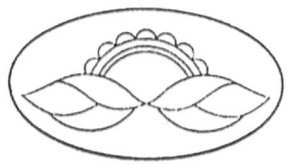

Sophia and I met when we were both doing secretarial work in a patent attorney's office in downtown San Francisco in 1947. Her talents were numerous, and while working with shorthand and typing, she also starred in the San Francisco Ballet.

Sophia had a profound effect on this farm girl from Yakima when she was hired at the patent attorneys' office where I had been the designated manager. On days when the patent applications were not overwhelming us, we talked about politics, religion, and the growing feminism in our culture. Her experiences were much more worldly than mine. Having been raised by a strong single mother, she had no difficulty voicing her opinions. I was single at the time and had only recently arrived in San Francisco.

One day, after I'd been married for six months, Sophia sat back in her desk chair and declared: "June, we are just as smart as these attorneys we work for. Why don't we go to law school?" I was dumbstruck at the idea, especially because my husband had just finished his law degree at Hastings Law School and I found the briefs I had typed for him very confusing. Even more important, I told her I was pregnant and found it very exciting.

Sophia continued to press forward with her idea of going to law school. One of the attorneys in our office picked up on her enthusiasm and helped her with her admission to Hastings College as one of four women in a class of 196 men. She graduated 3rd in her class but the local law firms weren't hiring women and she took a job as a law clerk for a California Supreme Court Justice.

The Supreme Court Justice for whom Sophia worked was so impressed with her skills and knowledge of law that he put in a word with Governor Ronald Reagan to appoint her to the Municipal Court. In 1974 she joined a nearly all-male bench. Every time Sophia was promoted in her professional life, she made sure that I was invited to her installation ceremony.

Although we saw little of each other for more than 20 busy years, the experiences we had shared kept our bond of friendship very strong. After her husband's death, Sophia moved to a retirement home very near me. I became concerned about her health when she began losing weight and seemed very frail, so she went to her doctor for a complete check-up. A week later she called to ask if we could have lunch.

"Of course," I replied, "But since you like my dog so much why don't I pick you up and bring you over here for lunch?" As we were sitting outdoors on my porch while she held the dog, Sophia announced that she had been diagnosed with pancreatic cancer. She immediately put her hand over mine and said, "Just listen for a minute because I want you to answer some questions for me and I don't need sympathy. I want to know how I can die gracefully because I have decided not to have surgery or any other treatment."

I had been prepared to hear what her doctor had said regarding her health but was taken by surprise at her announcement and the question that followed. My heart sank and for a moment I said nothing. When I had caught my breath, I reminded her that assisting someone else to die was illegal in our State. She laughed at me and reminded me that she was well aware of the laws but felt that she would not need anyone to assist her. A friend of hers had simply turned his face to the wall and died without accepting any medical treatment and she wanted to know how he did that. I reminded her that medicine was not my expertise but I had known someone who stopped eating and drinking in order to hasten their death. I knew that it was not necessary to remind her about unfinished business regarding legal papers and powers of attorney. After our light lunch, Sophia asked if

I would drive her back to her residence and promised to call me the next day.

As promised, she called to say that she had informed the management at her residence regarding her illness and they were moving her to a wing which included acute care and hospice care.

A few days later I had a phone call from her daughter. Jeanine and I had never had time to know each other well, but knowing Sophia, I was not surprised by the open dialog that followed.

"June, Mom said I should call you. She is not accepting food or drink and she wants me to talk to you." Her concern was very evident.

"Jeanine, I'm so glad you called. I'm sure it must be difficult for you in light of the diagnosis and your mother's decision to stop eating and drinking. This choice is rather new to me, too, but Sophia is the fourth person I have known to make this decision in the face of a diagnosis which is certain to be followed by death. I am glad to be able to tell you that it is a much more pleasant way to die than I have observed in my professional work with patients who pursue curative treatment for days, weeks, or months after being told by their physician that they cannot affect a cure.

"If Sophia's journey follows the others I have accompanied when they chose to die, she will be very comfortable and somewhat euphoric in a very short time. Although dehydration is thought to be something to strongly avoid, I've seen how easily the body stops functioning when all liquids and food are withdrawn. The lack of function leaves the patient very relaxed. What is most needed is that those around her continue to show their love and their support for the choice she has made."

My statement was followed by a brief silence.

"Well I see why she wanted me to call you. It sounds just like Mom, and of course I will support her even though it is hard to face this loss."

Sophia's doctor had agreed to her bringing in a hospice team to help educate her friends and family and closely follow her needs for "comfort" care. About a week later I went to visit and found her looking absolutely beautiful in a well appointed room on the ground floor where she looked out on a colorful garden. She smiled as she told me that she had not had food or liquids for 2 days.

As we visited, the Hospice doctor came through the door looking somewhat alarmed.

"Sophia, the nurses tell me that you are not eating or drinking. Don't you like being awake?"

Sophia rolled her eyes at me but said nothing.

From my own experiences in training hospice caregivers, I realized the doctor's question came from his sense of responsibility in supporting his patients but also in being sure they were aware of the consequences of their decisions. Although we had never met, we knew each other's positive reputations within our profession. So I turned to him.

"Doctor, Sophia has given this serious thought and does not want her final days to be spent pursuing life any further. She has made up her mind and is very much at peace with her decision."

Sophia had followed this exchange carefully and now turned to give the doctor a dazzling smile of affirmation. He visibly relaxed. After a few more minutes I excused myself and left them to discuss other matters.

I learned a short time later that her daughter, accompanied by her husband, had moved into Sophia's penthouse at the facility. As she slipped into a light coma, they continued to visit with her when possible and brought their children to extend their love and goodbyes to their grandmother. They also made sure that her close friends were aware of her impending death and had sufficient time to say their goodbyes.

Ten days after her death at the age of 88, on August 11, 2012, I went to her funeral mass in San Mateo which was attended by many friends and family as well as professionals from the Municipal and Superior Court bench in San Francisco.

TEN MONTHS LATER – THE INTERVIEW

I called Sophia's daughter, Jeanine, and asked if she was willing to talk to me about her mother's choice in dying. She was not only willing, but arrived at my home a few days later, her eyes full of sparkle. It was very interesting to discover that Jeanine and I both had similar enthusiasm and experience in knowing this woman who had been her mother.

She began by telling me the story of her husband's sister dying of pancreatic cancer just six months before Sophia received the same diagnosis. Sophia had never mentioned this to me. I found it extremely enlightening to know that Bob's sister had been taken in and out of the hospital numerous times, often in a state of emergency over about a six week period. They had also been aware of the aggressive treatments of surgery, chemo, and radiation, which often caused violent physical disturbance, only to be followed by more treatment in an attempt to prolong her life. The loss of this close relative and seeing her suffering as she died had never been mentioned in my conversations with Sophia. However, it clarified the certainty with which I watched Sophia make her own decisions. She had strongly disapproved of all the extreme measures that were taken in prolonging the life of her daughter's sister-in-law. Having observed and experienced this recent loss also helped the rest of her family understand why the matriarch of the family was following her own choices in the dying process.

Jeanine reported that the family had known Sophia was not feeling well. She had been having frequent stomachaches and was not eating well. When she paid a call on her doctor, he suggested some further investigation, but did not imply that he suspected anything very dangerous. Later, Jeanine felt the doctor had avoided communicating the seriousness of her mother's condition, not wanting to cause the family the inevitable pain. When she and her husband were shown the films of her mother's xrays, the doctor still did not suggest that what they were viewing was life threatening. She and I agreed that some doctors are not able to discuss the possibility of death because their training has focused on healing. Some of them have not considered death as a part of their personal lives either. However, in my professional work, I find that is rapidly changing and when Sophia was referred to an oncologist, the doctor sat down with her, told her the seriousness of her condition, and what her choices were.

Sophia immediately announced her diagnosis to her family and declared that she was considering what the oncologist had told her. It was at this time she lunched with me and we discussed her decision to end her life as gracefully as possible. She was 88 years old, had had a very successful, satisfying life and was fully aware of what the consequences of her decision would be.

As Jeanine and I talked, she reflected that the last few week of her mother's life had become a blur, but that she remembered her mother telling her to call me. We both felt that Sophia preferred not to tell her personally and face her daughter's anguish at hearing the news but that she needed to share the fact that she had already cut way back on her food and needed Jeanine's support in choosing this manner of dying.

Jeanine declared that she felt "blown away" by what was going on and found it hard to decide whether to focus on her mother's care and impending death, or her own shock at the loss she faced. She immediately knew that she could not urge food intake on her mother, even though that was her first impulse. She also knew that her mother had always been very decisive and always followed through on her decisions. When Sophia decided to do something, she did it well.

"When Mom was moved to the care unit in her living facility, my husband and I moved into her penthouse in order to have as much time with her as possible. We made our children aware of what was happening, which brought the comment, 'That sounds just like Grand-Mère.' The nurses who cared for Mom continued to make food available if she wished to eat but she only nibbled occasionally on watermelon."

Sophia died peacefully on August 11, just 32 days after being diagnosed. The family is at peace, although still mourning their loss, and is very pleased with the cooperation of her caregivers at the end of her life. However, Jeanine closed our conversation with her declaration that she is not sure she could do as her mother did. She added, "I love to eat too much."

CONCLUSION

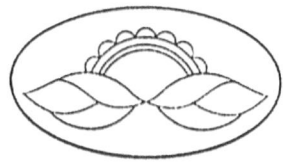

There are so many issues regarding death in America, that any change in our thinking about how we die will take some time to sort out. We are not only dealing with one of our most profound life experiences, but we are dealing with the accumulation of experiences that are different for all of us. What seems reasonable to many of us in withdrawing life support and stopping life saving measures, doesn't always deal with the feelings that accompany the actual carrying out of that decision. While the person dying may be very accepting of the process they are facing, the people surrounding them may have many opposing views. Every step in our evolution has happened only after prolonged persistence, from walking upright, to equality of the sexes. After a physical death, the living must process the lingering pain of grief but a healthy assistance in the death process can make grief much easier to process.

Many of us have not yet observed first hand the radical changes which have taken place with the advent of devices and drugs that can maintain physical life long after the patient is no longer mentally capable of making choices. New terms such as "brain dead" or "persistent vegetative state" are only recently in use with the arrival of modern technology. As the world has been made smaller and smaller by means of swift and inexpensive travel, religions have coalesced in their views of life and death, or taken opposing stances even more firmly.

Drug manufacturers have found profit in new medications which can cost hundreds, if not thousands, of dollars a week in a patient's fight for life. These manufacturers are supported by the strongest lobby group in Washington, D.C., and fight vigorously against any change in the present system.

Families stagger under the weight of watching a relative decline. As that relative becomes a stranger that they can no longer relate to, they find many reasons not to stop unremitting treatment that does not bring their loved one back. The fear of death and the religiously conflicted beliefs about God's will can leave caregivers paralyzed and focused on hope. It is true that there is no such thing as "false hope," but many think that it is not moral to hope for release from a wretchedly sick physical body for themselves or anyone else. We are cautiously beginning to allow "Physician Assisted Death" and California is the sixth state to pass this legislature.

The laws of cause and effect, which rule this planet, cannot be changed to favor individuals through prayer. Miracles are evidence of something that we do not yet understand but will eventually be found to be a part of those same laws. More current thinking is that, hoping for recovery when faced with dementia, stroke or brain damage, endless injections of morphine can be more cruel than the freedom of death.

If we have never reconciled that we must all eventually pass away and that our cozy family circle will be disrupted, we can suffer a lasting grief that becomes a calamity in our own healthy hold on life. Grief must be processed. We cannot avoid the pain; we must go through it. If feelings are repressed they constrict the body processes, including the immune system function. Many illnesses can result from un-processed grief. Talking in grief groups, one-on-one talk therapy or doing extensive writing about the feelings being experienced are all helpful. Learning that a loved one will always be a part of your life, through inner dialog or by creating a memory book can help us look back with gratitude that they shared a chapter or more in our lives.

Katy Butler's extensive research in writing her book, earlier referred to, reports that medical overtreatment costs the U.S. health care system an estimated $158 billion to $226 billion a year. One major study found that 13 percent of patients over eighty who underwent combined valve and bypass surgeries died in the hospital. In a smaller, confirming study, 13 percent died in the hospital and an additional 40 percent were discharged to nursing homes. It can be costly both emotionally and financially to enter this phase of life without considering the options available.

In the four stories I have told here, which I personally observed, it is clear that we can often claim our spiritual and moral authority by choosing how and when we die. Not always, because we are existing in a many-faceted culture. But we do not need to feel trapped in our physical body, unable to move on in our spiritual energy. As evidenced in the foregoing narratives, this can be wonderously helpful in allowing our families to go on after our physical death. Taking time to consider questions regarding our own death can lead to the true triumph of an accomplished life and the wonder or dying with peace and dignity